AMERICAN HOLIDAYS

★ ★

Independence Day

Jill Foran

Weigl Publishers Inc.

Published by Weigl Publishers Inc.
350 5th Avenue, Suite 3304
New York, NY USA 10118-0069
Web site: www.weigl.com

Library of Congress Cataloging-in-Publication Data

Foran, Jill.
  Independence Day / Jill Foran.
      p. cm. -- (American holidays)
Summary: Examines the history of Independence Day and describes some of the
ways that this holiday is celebrated.
Includes bibliographical references and index.
  ISBN 1-59036-109-1 (lib. bdg. : alk. paper) — ISBN 1-59036-165-2 (pbk.)
  1. Fourth of July--Juvenile literature. 2. Fourth of July
celebrations--Juvenile literature. [1. Fourth of July. 2. Holidays.] I.
Title. II. American holidays (Mankato, Minn.)
  E286.A1293 2004
  394.2634--dc21
                                        2003003954

Printed in the United States of America
1 2 3 4 5 6 7 8 9 0 07 06 05 04 03

Project Coordinator Tina Schwartzenberger **Substantive Editor** Heather C. Hudak
Design Terry Paulhus **Layout** Susan Kenyon **Photo Researcher** Barbara Hoffman

Photo Credits
Every reasonable effort has been made to trace ownership and to obtain permission to reprint copyright material. The publishers would be
pleased to have any errors or omissions brought to their attention so that they may be corrected in subsequent printings.

Architect of the Capitol: page 9T; **Corel Corporation:** page 17T; © **The Early American Digital Library:** pages 10, 12; **Getty
Images, Inc.:** pages 6, 15; **Independence National Historic Park:** page 13; **Map Resources:** page 7; **Peter M. Noyes of
Wapakoneta, Ohio:** page 18; **Bryan Pezzi:** pages 20, 21; **Photos.com:** pages 5, 11, 16; **PhotoSpin, Inc.:** page 22; **Ariel
Skelley/CORBIS/MAGMA:** page 3; **Jim Steinhart of www.planetware.com:** pages 9B, 17B.

Contents

Introduction

The United States of America was born on July 4, 1776.

Americans celebrate Independence Day on the Fourth of July. The United States was born on July 4, 1776. The country's leaders adopted a document called the Declaration of Independence on that day. The document declared that America was no longer under the control of the **British Crown**. It had become an independent country. The American people were free.

Independence Day is America's birthday party. Americans hold large celebrations with fireworks and music. They have picnics, watch parades, and spend time with family and friends. Most importantly, they celebrate their independence and freedom.

Some Americans wear clothing with the American flag or stars and stripes to show their national pride on Independence Day.

Thirteen Colonies

★ ★

People in the colonies wanted more freedom.

Until the mid-1500s, only Native Peoples lived in America. Then, Europeans began to travel to North America. Created in 1607, Virginia was the first English **colony**. Over the next 100 years, 13 colonies were formed in America. The British king ruled over all the colonies from 3,000 miles away.

People in the colonies wanted more freedom. They did not want a king to make their laws or force them to pay taxes. On September 5, 1774, leaders met in Philadelphia. They formed a group called the First Continental Congress. The group sent a list of complaints to the king.

★ ★ ★ ★ ★ ★ ★ ★ ★ ★
The first European colonists traveled to America on the *Mayflower*.

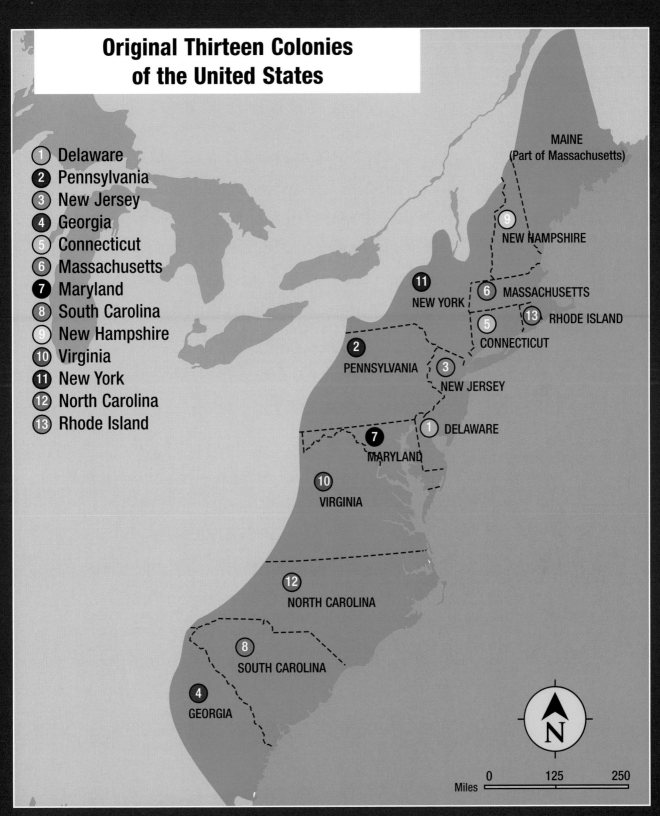

Original Thirteen Colonies of the United States

1. Delaware
2. Pennsylvania
3. New Jersey
4. Georgia
5. Connecticut
6. Massachusetts
7. Maryland
8. South Carolina
9. New Hampshire
10. Virginia
11. New York
12. North Carolina
13. Rhode Island

MAINE
(Part of Massachusetts)

9 NEW HAMPSHIRE

11 NEW YORK

6 MASSACHUSETTS

13 RHODE ISLAND

5 CONNECTICUT

2 PENNSYLVANIA

3 NEW JERSEY

1 DELAWARE

7 MARYLAND

10 VIRGINIA

12 NORTH CAROLINA

8 SOUTH CAROLINA

4 GEORGIA

N

0   125   250
Miles

The original thirteen colonies were Connecticut, Delaware, Georgia, Maryland, Massachusetts, New Hampshire, New Jersey, New York, North Carolina, Pennsylvania, Rhode Island, South Carolina, and Virginia.

7

Declaring Independence

★ ★

The colonists were fighting for independence from British rule.

DID YOU KNOW?

Although the colonies declared independence in 1776, the American Revolution lasted until 1783.

King George III did not want to give up control over the colonies. He sent soldiers to the colonies to help control any **rebellion** that might take place. This made the colonists angry. On April 19, 1775, American **patriots** and British soldiers began to fight. The American Revolution had begun. The colonists were fighting for independence from British rule.

American leaders held another meeting. In May 1776, the Second Continental Congress met in Philadelphia. The congress decided to write an official statement declaring the separation of the colonies from Great Britain. On June 11, a **committee** of five men was asked to write the declaration. On June 28, the committee presented a first **draft** to congress. The final draft of the Declaration of Independence was adopted on July 4, 1776.

Allyn Cox's painting *Writing the Declaration of Independence* hangs in the Great Experiment Hall in the U.S. Capitol.

The Declaration of Independence was signed at Independence Hall in Philadelphia, Pennsylvania, a World Heritage Site since 1979.

A Defining Document

★ ★

The colonists cherished the Declaration of Independence as a sign of their liberty.

Writing the Declaration of Independence was not an easy task. The document had to be very clear. All Americans had to agree with it. The five men assigned to draft the document were Benjamin Franklin, John Adams, Roger Sherman, Robert R. Livingston, and Thomas Jefferson. After the Declaration of Independence was adopted, it was distributed to the public. The colonists cherished it as a sign of their liberty.

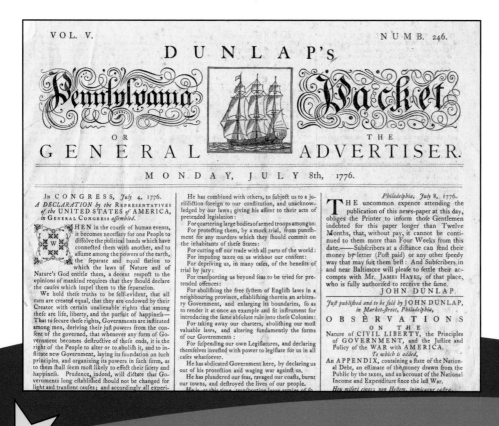

★ ★ ★ ★ ★ ★

The Declaration of Independence was published in newspapers so the American people could read it.

John Adams

John Adams helped write the Declaration of Independence. He also became the second president of the United States. For 8 years, Adams served as George Washington's vice president. In 1796, Washington **retired**. John Adams and Thomas Jefferson both entered the election for president. John Adams won the election by three votes.

We hold these truths to be self-evident, that all men are created equal, that they are endowed by their creator with certain unalienable Rights, that among these are Life, Liberty and the pursuit of Happiness.

—from the second paragraph of the Declaration of Independence

John Adams was one of the first people to suggest independence for America.

Creating the Holiday

★ ★

Crowds gathered to honor the birthday of their nation.

Once independence was officially declared, Americans wanted to celebrate. Crowds gathered at Independence Square in Philadelphia. The Declaration of Independence was read to the public for the first time on July 8, 1776. Bells rang out, music played, and people cheered.

DID YOU KNOW?

The United States Congress did not declare the Fourth of July a national holiday until 1941.

★ ★ ★ ★ ★ ★ ★ ★ ★ ★
Colonel John Nixon was the first person to read the Declaration of Independence to the public.

On July 4, 1777, exactly 1 year after the declaration was adopted, another celebration was held in Philadelphia. This time, crowds gathered to honor the birthday of their nation. They marked the occasion by firing cannons, lighting firecrackers, and dancing.

Fourth of July celebrations spread to other cities and towns. Americans wanted to honor the day they gained their independence from Great Britain. By the mid-1800s, everyone was celebrating Independence Day.

The Liberty Bell was rung after the first public reading of the Declaration of Independence.

13

Celebrating Today

★ ★

Many people attend picnics and eat summer foods.

DID YOU KNOW?

Traditional Fourth of July foods include hot dogs, hamburgers, corn on the cob, apple pie, and watermelon.

Today, Americans celebrate Independence Day in many ways. People do not have to work so they have time to spend with their families. They attend picnics and eat summer foods. They also take part in holiday events, such as baseball games, three-legged races, and pie-eating contests. Many communities host Independence Day parades. During these parades, crowds of people line the streets. They wave American flags as marching bands and beautiful **floats** pass them by.

After the Sun goes down on Independence Day, people gather to watch the fireworks displays. Most cities and towns across the United States set off fireworks on the Fourth of July. People gather at dusk to watch the fireworks light up the sky in bursts of red, white, and blue.

Crowds gather every Fourth of July in Washington, D.C., for Independence Day celebrations. Often, celebrations include concerts.

Americans Celebrate

I ndependence Day is celebrated across the country. This map shows a few celebrations that take place every year.

The people of Edmond, Oklahoma, celebrate Independence Day with a festival called LibertyFest. This 1-week festival features a Fourth of July parade, a car show, and kite competitions.

In Flagstaff, Arizona, Native Peoples celebrate Independence Day with a 3-day powwow. The powwow includes traditional dancing, drumming, and a rodeo.

Flagstaff, Arizona

Hundreds of people in Seward, Alaska, celebrate the Fourth of July by taking part in a 6-mile foot race. Racers try to make it to the top of Mount Marathon and back in less than 1 hour.

0   100   200   300 miles

Seward, Alaska

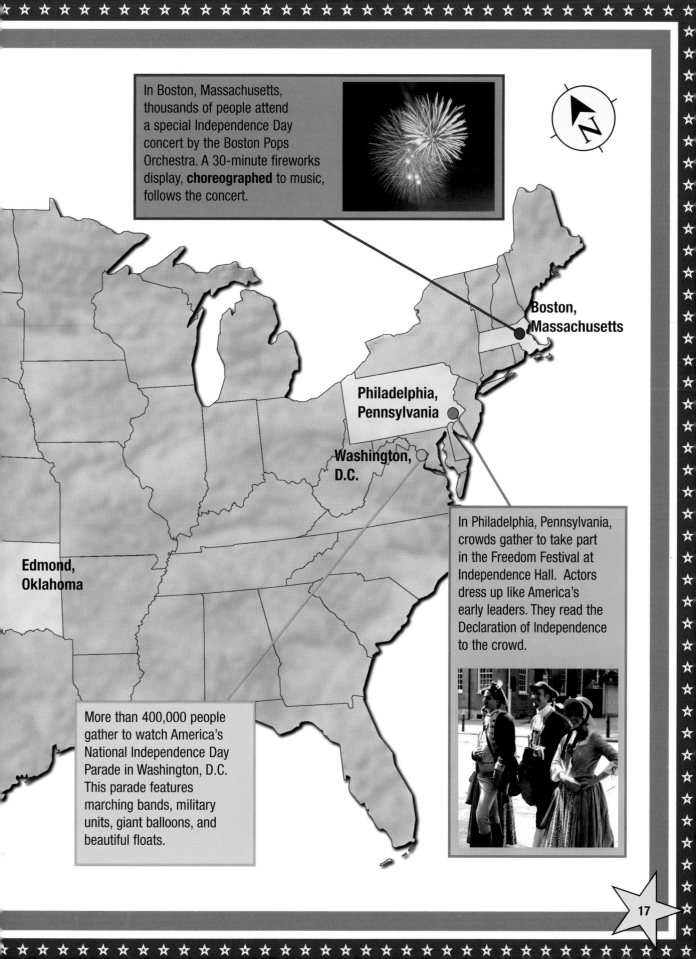

In Boston, Massachusetts, thousands of people attend a special Independence Day concert by the Boston Pops Orchestra. A 30-minute fireworks display, **choreographed** to music, follows the concert.

Boston, Massachusetts

Philadelphia, Pennsylvania

Washington, D.C.

In Philadelphia, Pennsylvania, crowds gather to take part in the Freedom Festival at Independence Hall. Actors dress up like America's early leaders. They read the Declaration of Independence to the crowd.

Edmond, Oklahoma

More than 400,000 people gather to watch America's National Independence Day Parade in Washington, D.C. This parade features marching bands, military units, giant balloons, and beautiful floats.

Holiday Symbols

Many people think of parades, fireworks, picnics, and summer holidays when they think of Independence Day. The holiday is a special celebration of freedom. Many national symbols help remind Americans of their freedom.

★ ★ ★ ★ ★ ★ ★ ★ ★

The stripes on the American flag represent the original thirteen colonies.

The American Flag

The American flag is displayed all over the country. Americans wave the flag at Fourth of July parades. The American flag is an important symbol of independence. Its design was adopted on June 14, 1777. The first flag had seven red stripes, six white stripes, and thirteen stars on a blue field. Since then, stars have been added to the flag as new states join the union. Today, the flag has fifty stars.

The Liberty Bell

The Liberty Bell was hung in the Philadelphia State House tower in 1753. For years, the bell rang to mark special occasions. On July 8, 1776, it rang to celebrate the adoption of the Declaration of Independence. In 1777, it rang to mark the first Independence Day celebration. In the mid-1800s, the Liberty Bell cracked. The bell was taken down from the tower. It is now at the Liberty Bell Pavilion in Philadelphia.

The Statue of Liberty

The Statue of Liberty stands in New York City, New York. This famous statue was a gift to the United States from France. The statue shows a woman escaping from the chains of **tyranny**. Her right hand holds a torch that stands for liberty. In her left hand is a **tablet** with the date July 4, 1776. On Independence Day, thousands of people visit the Statue of Liberty to celebrate the importance of freedom.

Further Research

Many books and Web sites have been developed to explain the history and traditions of Independence Day. Here are a few books and Web sites to help you learn more.

Web Sites

To learn about the history of Independence Day celebrations, visit:
www.fourth-of-july-celebrations.com

Learn more about the Declaration of Independence at:
www.ushistory.org/declarationBooks

Books

Cross Giblin, James. *Fireworks, Picnics, and Flags: The Story of the Fourth of July Symbols*. New York: Clarion Books, 2001.

Landau, Elaine. *Independence Day: Birthday of the United States*. New Jersey: Enslow Publishers, Incorporated, 2001.

Crafts and Recipes

Craft Stick Flag

There are many fun crafts you can create for Independence Day. For example, you can make a flag using craft sticks. To begin, paint five craft sticks red and four craft sticks white. Let the paint dry. Place an unpainted craft stick on a flat surface. Place this stick like a flag pole. Glue the painted sticks to the unpainted stick in an alternating pattern. You can use two broken craft sticks along the middle and left side to support the painted craft sticks. Next, cut a small square of blue paper. Cut small stars from the white paper, and glue them to the blue square. Glue the square to the corner of the craft sticks.

String of Stars

To create a string of stars, begin by drawing a large star on a piece of red, white, or blue craft paper. Cut out the star and decorate it with stars and stripes, just like the United States flag. Fold over the tip of the star, and glue it to a length of string. Repeat these steps to make more stars, and glue them to the same length of string. Be sure to leave extra string on each end so that you can hang your string of stars.

Independence Day Recipe

Red, White, and Blue Ice Cream Shake

Ingredients:

2 cups milk

vanilla ice cream

1 can of whipped cream

blue food coloring

ice cubes

red cherries with stems

red, white, and blue sprinkles

Equipment:

Ice cream scoop

Blender

1. With an adult's help, put two scoops of ice cream and 2 cups of milk in the blender. Blend for 30 seconds.
2. Add two ice cubes and a few drops of blue food coloring to the mixture. Blend for another 30 seconds.
3. Pour the mixture into a tall, clear glass. Add whipped cream, sprinkles, and a cherry to the top of the shake.
4. Enjoy your red, white, and blue ice cream shake.

Holiday Quiz

What have you learned about Independence Day? See if you can answer the following questions. Check your answers on the next page.

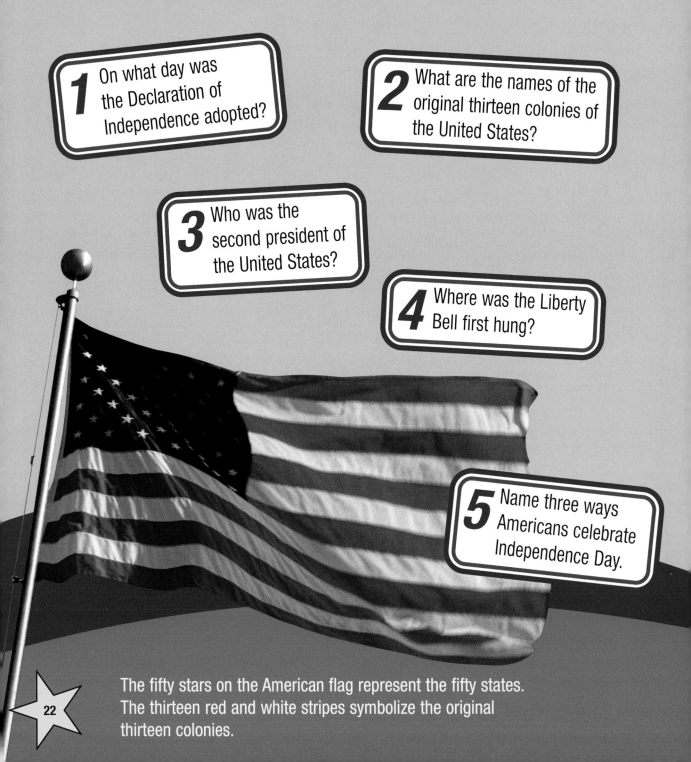

1 On what day was the Declaration of Independence adopted?

2 What are the names of the original thirteen colonies of the United States?

3 Who was the second president of the United States?

4 Where was the Liberty Bell first hung?

5 Name three ways Americans celebrate Independence Day.

The fifty stars on the American flag represent the fifty states. The thirteen red and white stripes symbolize the original thirteen colonies.

Fascinating Facts

★ The Declaration of Independence is on display at the Rotunda of the National Archives, in Washington, D.C.

★ The main author of the Declaration of Independence was Thomas Jefferson. He was chosen because he was the best writer on the Committee of Five.

★ Fifty-six American leaders signed the Declaration of Independence. All the leaders were very brave because they risked being arrested or killed for taking a stand against the British Crown.

★ On July 6, 1776, the Pennsylvania Post became the first newspaper to print the Declaration of Independence.

Glossary

British Crown: the government of Great Britain, ruled by a king or queen

choreographed: movement or patterns arranged to music

colony: a territory

committee: a group that is formed to act on something

draft: an early form of a written document

floats: low, flat platforms on wheels in parades

patriots: people who love their country

rebellion: fighting

retired: to stop working

tablet: pad of paper

tyranny: ruling unjustly

Index